PRAISE FOR RYZARD KRYNICKI

"A revelation. And a treasure. I thought I'd known most of the current Polish poets—but here was a glaring omission. He writes with an undercurrent of horror, and yet affirms the sacred, making me believe in the power of poetry to redeem us. As he writes, not without some irony, 'the world still exists.' The translations are superb."
   —Grace Schulman

"These are spellbinding poems: hieroglyphs, 'reports from the agents of secret reality,' traces left by the poet Issa reincarnated as a snail. In Clare Cavanagh's English, Ryszard Krynicki's Polish courts silence and flickers in paradox. It's a chaste and dire art: political, private, inviolable. I'm transfixed. Here's poetry doing its true work in two languages at once."
   —Rosanna Warren

"Part Issa haiku, part mystic speech, these delicate poems come from a time when men and women died for poetry. I almost feel unworthy of them, having never known the wall of fire and charred darkness of war. Please don't give these terse, clean poems short shrift—the little flames of purgatory have produced them."
   —Henri Cole

"There's nothing in English like these versions of this sharp, scary, un-ignorable Polish poet, whose decades of work speak, at the same time, to the privations and the frustrations of the unfree postwar state in which he lived and to the limits and ironies endemic to human life. If you have ever felt that 'we've outstripped everything, even the future'; if you have ever wanted to apologize to a moth, on behalf of the flame; if you find yourself having to say—or wanting your poets to say—'I'm not extinct'; if you want to know how short a universally applicable poem can get, or how to love shadows, or how to see past endemic grief—and whether or not you already follow Cavanagh's sharp translations of Krynicki's coevals—Krynicki may be a poet you need."

—Steph Burt

"Ryszard Krynicki lives with six cats, and I feel he must have captured some of the magic of those lithe creatures in his poetry. Krynicki must look into people the way that cats do. He must dream the way that cats see. Though his short poems are my favorites, his longer works are punctuated with lyrical acuity. This collected translation is a gift and I am blessed to have read it."

—Atticus Solomon, Literati Bookstore

Magnetic Point

Ryszard Krynicki

MAGNETIC POINT

Selected Poems 1968–2014

Translated, edited, and
with an introduction by
Clare Cavanagh

A NEW
DIRECTIONS
BOOK

Publisher's Note: New Directions gratefully acknowledges Drenka Willen's help with *Magnetic Point*.

Manufactured in the United States of America
New Directions Books are printed on acid-free paper
First published as a New Directions Book in 2017

Library of Congress Cataloging-in-Publication Data
Names: Krynicki, Ryszard, 1943– author. | Cavanagh, Clare, translator.
Title: Magnetic point : selected poems 1968–2014 / Ryszard Krynicki ; translated by Clare Cavanagh.
Description: First American paperback edition. |
New York : New Directions Publishing Corporation, 2017.
Identifiers: LCCN 2017013732 | ISBN 9780811225007 (alk. paper)
Subjects: LCSH: Krynicki, Ryszard, 1943– —Translations into English.
Classification: LCC PG7170.R9 A2 2017 | DDC 891.8/517—dc23
LC record available at https://lccn.loc.gov/2017013732

10 9 8 7 6 5 4 3 2 1

New Directions Books are published for James Laughlin
by New Directions Publishing Corporation
80 Eighth Avenue, New York 10011

In memory of our beloved friend
Stanisław Barańczak (1946–2014)

Table of Contents

FROM OUR LIFE GROWS (1978)

FROM NOT MUCH MORE (1981)

"Dusting Off Reality's Secret Face": the Poetry of Ryszard Krynicki

> *I was born in Austria during the war*
> *so my village schoolmates* from Poland *called me: Kangaroo.*
> *But usually for them I was Russky, Kraut, Jew.*
>   —Ryszard Krynicki, "Folk Etymology"

The complex history that Ryszard Krynicki compresses into this—typically terse and elliptical—late poem hints at the forces shaping the work of one of postwar Poland's greatest poets. Krynicki was born in "the place of death," as he writes in an early lyric, on June 28, 1943, in a Nazi labor camp in the town of Sankt Valentin, Austria, not far from Mauthausen. His parents, Polish peasants from Western Ukraine, served as slave laborers in the incongruously named *Nibelungenwerk*, the "third largest tank factory in the Reich."

After the war, his parents returned to a village once populated by Ukrainians, Poles, and Jews, and now part of the Soviet Union. His father, a new Soviet subject, was drafted into the Red Army, while mother and child were forcibly resettled to the so-called Reclaimed Lands, former German territories awarded to Poland after the war in compensation for the large swathe of eastern Polish territories absorbed into the Soviet Union. The family was reunited only two years later, in 1947.

This "ex-German" territory forms, we assume, the rural setting of "Folk Etymology." And this in turn suggests an answer to an unspoken question: why do the speaker's childhood tormentors come from a carefully italicized *Poland*? Unlike the speaker, their families were presumably transported to the newly Polonized territories from "true," central Poland, not from the ethnically suspect Ukrainian-Polish borderlands. Hence for the village boys "Austria" equals "Australia" equals "Kangaroo," and, by analogy, a child born in an Austrian labor camp to Polish parents from Ukraine is simultaneously "Russky," "Kraut," and "Jew." Some misidentifications stick: it is, I think, no accident that the two most recent editions of Krynicki's *Selected Poems* in Polish conclude with the words "*Shalom, achi!*"

Throughout his work, Krynicki is alert to the symbolically charged dimensions of the life that began under such unpromising circumstances. He is no less attentive to the problematic nature of a nation to which he both does and does not belong. In this shape-shifting "mobile country," with its historically mutable borders, one can go into exile simply by staying at home. "In this country? Yes, I stayed in this country. Exile comes in many shapes / and places," he writes in a poem from the late seventies.

"Folk Etymology" also reveals the acute linguistic and ethical sensitivity at work in the poetry. He quietly unpacks the troublesome paradoxes embedded in the fixed phrase he takes for its title. Folk etymology, the Oxford English Dictionary tells us, reveals the processes "by which the form of an unfamiliar or foreign word is adapted to a more familiar form through popular usage." The very term "folk etymology" (*etymologia ludowa*) comes tacitly under scrutiny in this brief lyric. In postwar Poland, the word "folk" (*lud*) suggests two separate, oppressive regimes. It evokes both the infamous *volk* glorified by Nazi Germany, and the Soviet-imposed *lud* of People's Poland (Polska Rzeczpospolita *Lud*owa), with its obligatory homage to dubious rural traditions: witness the rosy-cheeked peasants who on various patriotic occasions routinely performed the equivalent of mass, state-mandated square dancing.

The rural world of "Folk Etymology" is less picturesque, but no less preoccupied with defining and enforcing "Polishness." The childish persecutors are themselves victims two times over, first, of the Nazi occupation and then of the Soviet takeover. Displaced both historically and geographically, they can formulate a collective identity—what it means to be *from Poland*—only by taunting another child whose puzzling provenance allows him to play the role of various suspect outsiders. The newly Polonized territory these children inhabit has been stripped of the ethnic and religious minorities—by purges, transportations, mass atrocities, and forcibly redrawn borders—that had formed roughly a third of the interwar Polish population. How does a "folk," a people, reimagine itself after mass trauma? The little poem suggests a chilling answer.

Krynicki considers his poetic debut to be the collection *Act of Birth*, which appeared in 1969 in Poznan, where the poet had gone to study. The date is not accidental. With Adam Zagajewski and Stanisław Barańczak, Krynicki was a leading figure of what came to be known as the "Generation of '68" or "New Wave" of Polish poetry, a loosely affiliated group of young writers who came of age in People's Poland and found their voices in the wake of the political upheavals that marked the late sixties.

The young writers rebelled against both the political restrictions of the state and what they saw as the timidity and doublespeak of their poetic precursors. This reaction took two directions. While Zagajewski embraced the Krakow school of poetic "straight speaking," both Barańczak and Krynicki represented what came to be known as the Poznanian "linguistic school."

What did these schools mean in practice? The "straight speakers" strove to evade state doublespeak by "calling things by name," by stripping the veneer from a public language that bore little relationship to the reality of daily life in People's Poland. The "linguistic poets" took a different route. They explored what Krynicki called the "planet Phantasmagoria" of People's Poland by way of its verbal absurdities: "reality imitates the linguistic poetry/that irritates it," as he puts it in one poem of the 1970s. Hence passages like the following, from another poem of the period, "The World Still Exists":

> you go to work along Red Army Street
> the world still exists nothing has changed
> along the street's left side
> depending on where you're headed
> along with the entire nation
> along the leftist side
> along the street's ultraleftist side
> along its levitating side
> along its far-left wing
> you see a slogan the street's highest goal is man
> along the right etc. the slogan the street's highest
> you can't make out what's below
> raindrops airplanes snowflakes fall below
> nothing has changed
> cars slam the enigmatic letter &
> into the asphalt ...

Soviet language, Andrei Sinyavsky remarks, was not intended to serve as "a means of communication among people." It aimed to become "a system of incantations supposed to remake the world," or failing that, to provide "a substitute reality." Krynicki's distinctive brand of "socialist surrealism" draws on the incongruities between daily life in People's Poland and the ideology that claims to represent it. Hence the street the speaker takes to work each day, scrupulously renamed "Red Army Street" by the regime, cannot simply possess a right and a left side: it has a "leftist," an "ultraleftist," a "levitating" side, a "far-left wing."

Such work, needless to say, poses distinct challenges to the translator. In this case, the Polish language cooperated by providing Latinate roots for the wordplay that enables the street's left side to levitate by using its far left wing. In other cases it was less compliant. A key early poem, "Our Special Correspondent" (*Nasz specjalny wysłannik*, 1968), combines Polish morphology, spectacular puns, and geopolitics to remarkable, untranslatable effect. This did not stop the Polish censorship from passing judgment on the lyric. The regime cared deeply about subversive wordplay even when it couldn't understand it. The poem failed to clear the ominously named Bureau for Control of the Press, Publication, and Performance even after Krynicki strategically changed its title to "The Discovery of America." It was first published only a decade after its composition by the Paris-based publishing house Instytut Literacki.

Like Barańczak and Zagajewski, Krynicki was active both poetically and politically. The two fields of activity converged in multiple ways. The great dissident Adam Michnik speaks of the political and cultural "climate created by the poetry of Barańczak, Krynicki, and Zagajewski." The generation's poets "worked out a new language for its conversation with reality: we ceased to be slaves of others' words." Krynicki's work appeared chiefly in censored or underground editions, or in émigré presses—the so-called "second circulation"— through the seventies and eighties. Still, his elliptical, punning politics managed to rile the authorities time and again. Krynicki was at different points arrested on trumped-up charges, dismissed from work, and forbidden from publishing. Even his name was banned for a while from official publications.

Both Barańczak and Zagajewski left Poland in the 1980s. After the declaration of martial law in December 1981, Barańczak was not allowed to return from the United States, where he had accepted a teaching post at Harvard. Zagajewski emigrated to France in the mid-eighties for personal reasons, and returned to Poland permanently only decades later. Only Krynicki continued his poetic and political activity under the restrictions and privations that marked the final decade of People's Poland. He was "unfit for exile," he remarks ruefully. But he also suffered from what he calls the "unsettlement complex" that kept him from accepting any seemingly stable status quo, whether officially imposed or oppositional. This mixture of engagement and distance marked the distinctive poetic voice that emerges in this decade. Krynicki increasingly turned to a stripped-down, gnomic poetry that was widely circulated in the underground. Two brief lyrics of the period read as follows:

I Can't Help You

Poor moth, I can't help you,
I can only turn out the light.

Facing the Wall

A woman turns the mirror

to face the wall: now the wall
reflects the dead snow
crunching under iron soles.
The fire freezes.
Nothingness affixes bayonets.

Stanisław Barańczak and I began our decades of collaboration with Krynicki's poems of this period, some of which appear here in our translations from the mid-eighties. The political implications of such poems would have been clear enough to Polish readers at the time. But Stanisław would have been the first to warn against reading them as purely political. Krynicki possessed, as Stanisław told his students (of whom I was one), "the greatest lyric gift of his generation."

Compression, mysticism, wit: these are trademarks of Krynicki's poetry from his earliest work to the present. He is Poland's greatest translator of Paul Celan and Nelly Sachs, who rank among his masters, alongside poets ranging from Kobayashi Issa to Guillaume Apollinaire and Zbigniew Herbert. He shares his spiritual and ethical concerns with Zagajewski and Barańczak—an anthology of the three writers might easily take its title from Zagajewski's well-known poem "Mysticism for Beginners."

But you'd never mistake one poet for another. Krynicki is unparalleled in his respect for, and, complex engagement with, the white space on the poetic page:

> Nothing, night beyond the glass
> looks through me with the nongaze
> of the boy I was, am
>
> not, won't be.

So reads one little poem from the late eighties in its entirety. The nothingness that stares with no one's gaze also lingers just outside the poem's miniature frame. Like Szymborska, another of his masters, he is a specialist in the infinite varieties of "nothing" that surround us in poetry and life alike. "There is so much Everything / that Nothing is hidden quite nicely": Szymborska's lines from "Reality Demands" might easily be the epigraph to Krynicki's writing. Like Szymborska, he is also an extraordinarily acute observer of what is. His relentless, ethically charged attention shapes the distinctive brand of surrealism he draws from daily life:

> shop sign "World of Stockings" in Gliwice
> the shout "you dumb fuck" carried like a banner
> in a certain town on a certain morning
> "Zygmunt Krasiński's posthumous relations
> with a certain soul" in the local library,
> the calculus of probability,
> the invasion of monuments,

"Report on the Blind," the evening dailies,
"Proof that Napoleon Never Existed" ...

(from "Parting, Decline")

Stairs, moving sidewalks, Europe, stairs.
Watch for unattended luggage.
Front page headline:
"Hauptgewinn: Ein Baby."

(from "Munich Airport: In Transit")

The infinite imperfectability of poetry and life alike is one of the poet's great themes. But "mistakes in art can be corrected, it's different in life," he notes. He is a meticulous editor of his own and others' work, as his magnificent editions of Zbigniew Herbert's writing demonstrate. I've watched him instantly locate and correct the typos in an early, underground edition of his poems I found in a Warsaw used book kiosk.

Poetry, infinity, emptiness, and the traces of a palpable, impurely human existence converge in a late poem on editing the manuscripts of a vanished poet, presumably Herbert:

The old poet's frail manuscripts
bear traces of ash, countless cigarette
holes, coffee stains, less often,
red wine, and now and then
the almost unintelligible prints
of cat paws, vanishing

into spacetime.

CLARE CAVANAGH

•

Magnetic Point

Act of Birth

born in transit
I came upon on the place of death

the cult of the individual unit
of measures
and weights

the military unit

progressive paralysis
paralyzing progress

each day I listen to
the latest news

I live
in the place of death

*

and in winter when a stable of snowdrifts drew close in a sudden influx
of crushed glass,
and in summer, when the eyelids of fruit closed over flowers
(a precipice of rain mimicked fallen walls)

the journey dragged on like falling from a tall bridge; un-
ending, though constrained by sleep and decomposing sentences,

sentences not to be written

*

dawns, daybreaks, secret signs,
a journey like reading a foreign book
about familiar places,
startled from wakeful sleep on the world's unnumbered page,
I read this journey backwards in an unknown tongue

*

naked, I awoke abruptly in a bread line,
abruptly naked at religion class in church,
in a fourth grade lesson on the earth's roundness,
I awoke abruptly at an unknown station,

awoke abruptly
to stray?

to go

*

That sudden night was full
of salt and resin, the grace of eyes and lips,
darkness crouched in the lamp's small church
my body took shelter in yours,
saw in the dark.

Beneath the dew's eyelids unpeopled pupils
of mist dreamed,

wounded childhood ebbed.

*

Through skin we live
too close to draw near: that separation,
through men, whom you recall in me, endures,
through men, who once paced you, the railway
station of a text in a foreign tongue, through women,
whom I didn't win enough to forget; only
that first-born fear, we recognize each other by it like
a native tongue in an unknown station; closest, so
most distant, dearly hated,
two foreign grafts growing from the same stump, from
the cut trunk of a glance, a broken conversation, a spear
pierced two beasts, the beasts of breath, that
caught in our throats: spear? breath? even if
you graft it, expect no
tree but sleeplessness; we live through skin too distant
to speak of separation; it went on between us like a drawn-out trip
when the train is late and you must wait
alone at the empty stop
with a chance stranger; it went on between us? that close
distance, that first-born pain and breath
diminished to a gasp; yes and sight was between us; we live

through the skin of glimpses.

*

Leave me a wisp of hair, the track of your refusal,
a wisp of hair at least if you can't miscarry
blood, a wisp of blood, from a journey circulating
over pathless tracks of separation, unpeopled
greetings, save
the child
from sleep, a wisp of kiss,

lose it, leave it, release it.

*

if I'm true to anyone—I'm true to you
if I betray anyone—I betray you
if I long for anyone—I long for you

if I am just an echo shadow from your sleep
if I forget anyone—how could it be you

*

so let us try once more to play at open
doors, at two fires: childhood and war, conjoined
in ashes. Childhood's ashes are behind us, before us a double flame,
unreadable; just the same, let us read from the fire, from that
extinguished lifeline, let us read, dead inside, like the tongues
of vanished generations. Tongue of flame, illicit child
of two fires, what remained to us,
you childless line, book of ashes, mute
answer so uncertain that I can believe you. And don't
try to outstrip yourself, childless word, flame's unreadable
initials in a cuneiform
of traces
on polar snows,
desert sands. Posthumous child, child
in vain; you've scarcely risen from your knees
when you become a curse.

*

on the foothills of an abyss
on a slope of lightning your house once stood

Living Poetry

Poetry is
like blood transfused for the heart's work:
the donors may have died long since
in sudden accidents, but their blood
lives—and merges with other bloodstreams,

and resuscitates other lips.

*

tenderness—as if in some deserted house you'd found
a cluster of hair on a cut sheet
and a strand of violets fading in a vase

lies—in the fatally wounded arriving
on islands that the living do not know,
in a child's ribbon saved from a pogrom

He Who Chooses Solitude

in memory of Tadeusz Peiper

He who chooses solitude—will not be alone.
He who chooses homelessness—will have the world's roof overhead.
He who chooses death—will not cease living.
He whom death chooses—will die

slightly

If Love

If love outgrows us,
then parting becomes our native tongue
suddenly overheard in unknown stations.
Only the astonishment that seizes
us while reading a love letter's relics,

only the parting that stuns us:
born not of love, but hatred,
for which departure means return.

SEPTEMBER 1969

To ...

tenderness as harsh as parting:

you—don't even talk in your sleep
I—hold my peace even in sleep

between us lies not a sword but blood—conceived
fear lies between us
our talk echoed only in murmuring doves
(will the white dove's whisper lift this heavy load?)
as if you were my wife and my only child
blood of my blood
fatal illness
free verse
talking with you draws the world near
talking with you withdraws the world

as close as dawn

Don't Cry

Don't cry—crying breeds false angels,
don't smile—smiling breeds false demons,
don't wish to die—the dream will mirror you
in its vast stillness

and we will both be silent

Now That I Know

Now that I know you didn't die:

the grind of a braking tram, the telegram,
a sharply shattered glance, the dream about a bloodless child,
the weather forecast and—whatever happened

now that I know it's not you,
they speak of someone else to others, strangers, kin,
in graying voices

they become mirrors

OCTOBER 1970

Posthumous Journey (I)

she combs her illuminated, endless
hair before a graying mirror
as if running sleeplessly through her—
another's body, burning sacrifice, in dreams,
astray
in a white blizzard of skin that surrounds,
confines, unbinds her

the mirror, reflected nothingness, gray with terror,
the light of extinguished stars
gazes with her stranger's eyes
and the moment, blind and second-sighted, doesn't pass,
when it alone is: from hunger pangs
a precisely polished surface
of glass
or metal
emerges, grows

and she, doubly dead in separation,
in haste, as if afraid of missing
the last tram

combs her hair

Posthumous Journey (II)

Born in the place of death,
awakened suddenly from nonexistence,
you will be your own comrade in exile,
whom can you summon for help,
not knowing your own guilt
awaiting punishment

Blind—second-sighted as sometimes comes from dreams,
as if you'd regained your sight just to see
the scene and never forget it.
Unlinked from the dark light of woman's blood
and tossed into the world,
the womb's fruit: belly and element, fatal fruit
(death is unambiguous,
unambiguity is deadly):
"Who will cry with your tears,
with whose tears will you see?"
You awoke from blind sleep to read:
remain,
remain an honorary donor of blood, semen, and bone,
remain, remain,
and challenge no one but yourself,
and affirm only your own existence,
which

undoes you.

Door

Empty word, unpronounceable word: time. So
you didn't recall that language in time and stayed
in the shadow of a tree's
door. In a forest of ashes, in a wilderness of dust
you met friends
with the eyes of trees. In an opening door the features
of a face. A woman of the night embodied you. In a forest
of the dead, in a forest of dead tongues
your manuscript vanished,
you couldn't find it: that side
of the world, a card just torn,
could no longer be deciphered. What remained, an empty
word: time,
an unintelligible page

in the indictment.

From a Distance

from Max Hölzer

Frail foam on the ripples of a river
that never reached the earth's surface. Settling
on the sand. On the shield of a blind
sun.

Ants arrayed for war
stalemated on the shore in a matched battle:
a man and a woman sunk in each other as in sleep. Covered
only by open wounds.

Around their bright bodies
tiny Hosts arise. As if
a dancing couple
cast in glass had shattered.

Island of Death
(Song)

from a painting by Henryk Waniek

Death gives birth to you, and for all of us on earth
death is our parent;
death perishes,
death is resurrected
in another's dream, which is your waking.

Sons of one death and many elements,
we are all children.

Don't let fear frighten you; it works without ceasing
to make your animal death human.

Look into the pulsing mirror of sleep,
death ripens in your heart and mouth
like the transience that outlasts you.

Death lives with you, it sleeps with you like a sister.
Death lives in you, dies with you.

Parting, Decline

accidental witness to my own decline,
banished from my own skin and another's heart
"The void that fills my house is so immense"
oh Kościańska Street
and a vision of the street,   \
shop sign "World of Stockings" in Gliwice
the shout "you dumb fuck" carried like a banner
in a certain town on a certain morning,
"Zygmunt Krasiński's posthumous relations
with a certain soul" in the local library,
the calculus of probability,
the invasion of monuments,
"Report on the Blind," the evening dailies,
"Proof that Napoleon Never Existed,"
my "Act of Birth" and not my proof of death,
proof that Stalin
(hence the criminal's apparition
in an oneiric poem,
Moscow "Pravda," Warsaw "Inside Story"?),
the moon's influence on a woman's life,
books, countries, unknown tongues,
I outstripped my sole life long ago,
the world and I take leave each evening,
like it or not,
you had to lie,
you had no friends,
no adversaries,

no master,
no disciples,
women, yes,

the moon's dark breath,

partings and declines

The line "The void that fills my house is so immense" is from Jan Kochanowski's *Laments*, as translated by Seamus Heaney and Stanisław Barańczak (Farrar Straus & Giroux, 1995)

Opening

On the morning of May 1, 1969,
in a compartment of an express train, Warsaw—Vienna,
I'm reading in turns *Regio*, a volume by Tadeusz Różewicz, the
    contemporary Polish poet,
and the short course of train schedules headed
from a worse past into a bitter future,
the girl sleeping across from me
can't master her spreading knees,
knees close, mouth opens,
mouth closes, knees open
as if talking in her sleep,
knees close, mouth opens,
mouth closes, knees open,
like a faux pas, a tongue's slip,

but that's not the point, that women too
perform certain actions mechanically

a surreal gateway between us
a purple cavalry in pursuit

but that's not the point, that certain associations are mechanical

(a dream within a dream, someone's mother, fleeing,
women and horses, an angel,
the secret tongue in which he warned me)

the customs officer, opened my leather suitcase
(it was pigskin, top quality,
exported exclusively
to underdeveloped countries),
and discovered the remains
of my book
and many other insoluble matters

—I don't like that pigskin—he announced loudly—
—we'll see what you mean to say by this—

How I Lost My Virginity

At an unspecified time on an indeterminate day:

at an unspecified time on an indeterminate day
the book I'd put on the sill fell from the church
window. I ran downstairs, lost my way,
and obeyed the summons of an unknown man: Follow
me! —Here at my first confession I
couldn't admit to the sin of
parthenogenesis. The stranger gave me a phosphorescent hand
lopped off at the wrist. A streak of sky-blue light
drew from the darkness his bared chest,
carelessly concealed
beneath a black jacket, the kind worn in these parts
only on special occasions: marriage, a conversation
meant to reduce the term for obtaining a cooperative apartment
from ten years to eleven, graduation,
or a funeral. We genuflected
before the main altar, on which the condemned divinity
forgave a harlot. At that moment, I would rather have had fear
consume me than go for further testing. The side walls
held two times six blaspheming pictures
and countless votives, the whip of a well-lit
tsaress, the golden pen with which the brilliant linguist
had signed death sentences. —But I'm not
Origen—my guide warned me
unexpectedly, and just as we exited,
he climbed into a nearby taxi. Once more I was left

alone
and seeking my lost book in vain,
I tried to return. After a few steps
I began sinking in the boggy terrain. It was the wrong
church. All the windows and doors (bearing the number 69
which recalled the sign for Cancer and also a certain hotel
room, booked with some difficulty) had been boarded up. The police
came running, the special unit for travel control, and a girl
under the sign of the Snake, whom I'd long since managed
to forget, cried—He is mine!—reproaching
me for my faults and hands

amputated in delirium

The Tongue Is Wild Meat

to Mr. Zbigniew Herbert
and Mr. Cogito

The tongue is wild meat that grows in wounds,
in the open wounds of lips, feeding on truth belied,
the tongue is a bared heart, a naked blade,
it is defenseless, the gag that stifles
uprisings of words, it is a tamed beast
with human teeth, it is the inhuman that grows in us
and outgrows us, the red flag we spit out
with the blood, the split that engulfs us, the
true lie that seduces,

the child, who, learning truth, truly lies.

And We Really Didn't Know

to Adam Michnik

Maybe we were children, we lacked experience,
we only knew we'd been forced to believe in lies
and we really didn't know what else we wanted
besides respect for human rights and truths,
when we gathered in the small square
before the monument to the great poet
who spent his youth in a captive nation
and the rest of his life in exile,

we lit cigarettes and lying newspapers,
we lit cigarettes, though they poisoned our bodies,
we lit newspapers, since they poisoned our minds.
we read the constitution and the declaration of rights,
and we really didn't know that human rights
might end by contradicting
the rights of citizens,

and we really didn't know,
that armored cars could be sent against the helpless,
against us, who were still children
armed only with ideas that we'd been taught in schools,
and that the same schools had untaught us,
and we really didn't know
that they could all be elided
by the ruthless onslaught of sated force,
by the multiplied lie,

and we really didn't know that the adults believed not us,
but the multiplied lie, that everything can be elided,
everything can be forgotten
then everything goes on as if nothing had happened,
and we really didn't know that memory is the citizen's foe,
and we really didn't know, that living here and now
meant pretending to live elsewhere, in other times,
and to oppose at best the shadows of the dead

through an iron curtain of clouds

My Wife Fights to Protect Man's Natural Environment

My delicate wife fights to protect
man's natural environment.
Mornings her slim body vanishes in clouds
of soot and sulphur, on streets giving birth
to cars and hunger, to nooks in skyscrapers
ceaselessly breeding large families,
among mines and mills, in the spasmatic depths
of a city built from rust and concrete, crawling,
motionless, like a gray glacier. I look for her in vain
—then suddenly I find her, lost, in a train
(am I lost? fleeing myself?)
and through the thick raster I scarcely recognize
her uncertain smile in the group photograph
illustrating a labored feature on new methods
of protecting the environment in the local paper,
which once more promises iron and coal,
a car, a new steel mill, and a Poland of sorts

for every family. Ours too, alas.

My Friend Cuts Himself Off from the World

My friend, about whom I know only
that he's someone else,
lies down on the bed and covers his face with a newspaper,
cuts himself off from the world;
his body becomes the body of someone
for whom he is just now
dying in a dream;
the newspaper covers him like a shroud,
it kisses his lips,
his lips
sip print,
print drinks his blood,
the newspaper, sated with his blood,
drops to the floor

and recovers:
pale as parchment

The Catastrophist of 1972

The catastrophist of 1972 returning home one morning
sees workers surging from the station's throat
and people who arrive for delegations and professional workshops,
their briefcases bulging with unfulfilled dreams;
he takes from his heart's left pocket the bill for the light
and the gas with which he'd meant to kill himself,
but remembered just in time that he'd miss the meeting
for collectors of colorful dreams;
from his heart's right pocket he takes a ticket for improper crossing
of life's road on planet Phantasmagoria,
which on earth may entitle him
to free trips on the state-run railways;
from his heart's right pocket he takes his inflatable double,
which he places each day behind his desk,
from the left—the key to distinguishing the friends of animals
from his wife's friends;
from his left profile he's a demon adept at quick changes of skin,
from the right—the man of your life, Krystyna;
with his left eye he sees his shadow reflected in the window
of Literary Publishers,
with the right—a pure idea that strolls along streets creeping
    sluggishly

and so on

White Flag

White flag,
white flag of sheets,
white flag of the hospital,

white flag in the blood,
white flag of a crowd,
white flag of hope,

yes, yes, I surrender,

you beat too strongly,
you beat too impurely, heart

Tadeusz Peiper

The shadows are equal in the morning and evening
but lie on different sides of the tree
Tadeusz Peiper believed in the mission of the new art. He suspected
that rivals lay in wait for his ideas. They sent false
emissaries, women, the seductive agents of other
literatures, speed demons, vampires armed with invisible
claws who suck a man's
thoughts and rhythm from him, they lull his vigilance with downy
featherbeds of praise, they drown mimesis in downpours
of saliva. They can turn themselves
into carbon paper, a false bottom, the copy of a lost poem,
they prompt false prophecies. They exit others' mouths
as "New Mouth," give birth to others' children, who shout
"A." They impersonate Stanislaw Ignacy Witkiewicz—he
avoided Zakopane so as not
to meet him, he went to Krynica. But even here
his own features in another's face distressed him, x-rays
sent through unidentified objects. Unemployed people
didn't read poems, the prosecutor and secret police did,
to be sure, in their peculiar way. The veal chop
came to life beneath his knife, it tasted like a flag, foodstuffs
secreted lethal poison.
Tadeusz Peiper believed that art orders
chaos, it's useful in life. On the first day of the war
(which is a woman)
he wanted to seal his windows and tore the two portaits Witkacy
had drawn into strips. (He thinks of him then:

my friend and comrade in the battle for new art). Useless,
the cardboard was too stiff, besides he lacked
the thirteen pennies to buy paper. The number thirteen (which
is a woman) once more bared its diabolic
face. Witkacy put back the razor. The new art (which is
a woman)

didn't fit with life.

(FROM AN UNWRITTEN EPIC)

Flood

Morning's specter, rumpled sheets,
letters stopped short on reason's
border, poisoned newspapers and marked cards,
the results of secret ballots and future
elections, reports from the agents of secret reality.
typescripts of books written for others'
desk drawers, new speeches (what's old
is new again), meat, the battleship Potemkin,
tapes from secret taps and the literature of labor, vodka, and the
      censor's
files, the wreck of a radio jammer (oblivion's
ideal apparatus), extraterrestrial signals,
red ID papers and nylon flags,
youth reserve corps, reservations
for young writers (eliminate the
extraneous), portraits unhung, health
updates, and the Kremlin mummy,

all this flowed
poured toward our mouth

approached our throat

The Fascists Change Shirts

The fascists change shirts again.
They change black shirts for white hours,
for the white spots in the posthumous newspapers of a deserted
      town,
from whose pages all traces have been purged of the blood
that wasn't made into a banner.

The shattered brain of an animal crushed by tank treads,
the shattered brain of a coast,
the shattered brain of an ocean,
the shattered brain of a makeshift world,
the fascists change shirts again,
their own and their victims'.

On white shirts the traces of brain are less perceptible,
on black shirts the traces of blood are less perceptible.

The fascists change the posthumous shirts of a makeshift world
      again
and take from the cloakroom their protective black-and-white
banners,
which are often false even as obituaries

For Some Time

For some time now I've noticed
that when an owner whistles for his dog

most passersby turn around.

March 31, 1971, 7:21 p.m.

the whole world watches Moscow

12,100 people watch a match in Idraetspark Stadium
Manchester City leads 1-0 after Young's goal
(automatic association with *Night Thoughts*)
everything may still be regained
(freedom? equality? fraternity?)

the unity of words and deeds
startles on unpeopled streets
saved from a heart attack the miner feels fine
and the lady who knows everything
(since she sells newspapers)
thinks he'll go down in history
coal refuses to give up its comrade's body
and at a different hour
but the exact same time
Charlie Manson
waiting for death in the gas chamber
(automatic association with)
forecasts universal bloodshed

the whole world watches Moscow

a fan of the Zabrze Miner Team dies of someone else's heart attack
a militant civilian exits
the Violation Bureau

of the civic militia headquarters
it's pay day
no alcohol is sold today and even so
a stray passerby
who must not have a TV yet
is singing that you zapped the clap I
argue about Peiper with a poet? a critic? from Warsaw
who had to postpone his reading
since now

the whole world watches Moscow

one survived
ten miners perished
on the Coast
the dead were buried secretly
we hold our tongues

the whole world
watches Moscow
the nation
over the past
under the leadership
has once again achieved vast
The Worker's Tribune will hire a proofreader
(eternal future)

it's nearly 7:22
everything may still be regained
(faith? hope? love?)
confusion continues in the Miner's defense

the whole world is fighting
in Gdańsk
quintuplets were born
the press puts pressure
reporters can't be bought
but keep getting raises
newspapers are purchased
raining in Copenhagen
high time
to quit smoking
we hold our tongues
the nation-wide debate rages on

Posthumous Journey (III)

One fine morning
you too may suddenly leave home,
never to return

to the home you never had.

You may wake up at Central Station in Warsaw,
a city where twenty years ago
ten rats still replaced each occupant
and polyvinyl chloride currently replaces steel,
one occupant occupies a second occupant,
the third a fourth (and vice versa), at the station of a city
that holds no irreplaceable people, at a station
from which, if warning signs can be believed,
there is "No Exit" (and now there's no sign either),
maybe in front of the factory gates, the factory
whose walls hold the victims of December's tragedy
alongside our shared public secret,
decaying, still incompletely born,
though it designs the blueprint for its own gravestone
within the confines of art therapy;
maybe on red square
from the blood of reds, whites, grays, unidentified
(but all identically defenseless)
that was pedantically covered with sand
(the sand's gone too; snow hid it,
wind scattered it, rain spread it);

maybe on the outskirts, in front of the worker's hotel
facing a slogan
"The press hastens progress" (word three is missing the first *s* and
       the *n*);
maybe in a theater at a current comedy,
when the actress lost her mind
(at the same time that tanks set off in a specified
direction
to hasten the progress of a friendly hatred
for the sake of the peace and security of a citizen gray with dust
who may at any moment become a moving target),
while trying to free herself from a flaming caftan, the safety
of her superficial skin,
her shallow sex, her deep defeat
on unfeeling lips;
you wake up wherever,
forgetting your name, your parents' names,
your place of birth, your country, the faces of false friends
beneath your successive faces, with sand under eyelids,
with a numb tongue
and a blinded heart;
just then the radio may issue an announcement
about someone who left suddenly and still hasn't returned,
someone who looks deceptively like you,
as attested by the stamps
in his proof of personal nonentity, the military
service book (which, if you happen to be male,
will remember you even when
everyone else has forgotten), the savings book
of a wasted life and the separate body of someone
you no longer wish to meet,

but can't evade, you pick up
the picture that you dropped,
the photo of a strange woman
smiling at your strange child,
the tanks will creep towards the border
of a friendly violence,
at every step posters will warn
about "Venereal Diseases on the Move,"
tanks will counterattack, women will receive better
working conditions in the quarries
of the immediate future, while the youngest poets
will be protected from the parataxis now rampant in poetry;
you may need to explain
in chance encounters with the doubles of nonacquaintances
that you know nothing about the fate of a still unborn
past that can't detect its shape
or its place in our life, the past-axolotl,
giving birth in solitude
following the most recent abortion of the brain,
you may meet Jan Palach,
a twenty-something-year-old boy from Central Europe,
just your age,
who voluntarily self-immolated in the mobile crematorium
of aid carried on bayonet blades
to maps of future borders, you may meet him,
the occupant of the equally tragic country
from which your mobile country
received Christianity centuries ago;
you may meet the twenty-something-year-old Rafał Wojaczek,
who never came back,   ·
you may meet Tadeusz Borowski,

Andrzej Bursa, Marek Hlasko, who all outgrew their own hearts,
the sinful saints of your youth,
when you sought truth—instead of understanding,
when you sought truth—instead of justice,
when you sought truth—instead of hope,
when you sought truth—instead of faith,
you may meet an amused Soso Dzhugashvili,
who was also a child once,
and maybe Judas, hapless prophet of provocateurs,
whom no one even wanted to crucify,
so he hanged himself from the cord of a busy classified phone,
you may meet no one
among party members and nonmembers, believers and nonbelievers,
you may meet workers from the universe's coast
with tongues shot through,
with stigmata on their shot foreheads,
you may meet no one, you may meet disappointment,
which never lets you down,
you may meet no one
as you too suddenly depart from the Children's, Men's, Old People's
    Home

never to return.

The World Still Exists

nothing changes
you wait each day for an apartment allocation
you wake up the world still exists
you come back from work the world still exists
you read the paper
the Chinese have discovered a bone
that may revolutionize science
and refute Darwin's theory
you go to bed drift off
before catching all the latest news
you sleep dream nothing
you wake your bones won't revolutionize science
you go to work along Red Army Street
the world still exists nothing has changed
along the street's left side
depending on where you're headed
along with the entire nation
along the leftist side
along the street's ultraleftist side
along its levitating side
along its far left wing
you see a slogan the street's highest goal is man
along the right etc. the slogan the street's highest
you can't make out what's below
raindrops airplanes snowflakes fall below
nothing has changed
cars slam the enigmatic letter &

into the asphalt
time flows in immobility like an electrical current

but your child coming home from preschool already knows
the the highest goal is

etc.

Citizens of Phantasmagoria

to Zdzisław Beksiński

Citizens of Phantasmagoria,
we long ago surpassed the speed of light,
we catalyzed our planet
and converted it into an unidentified flying object:

we've outstripped everything, even the future.

We keep growing younger,
the objects, animals, and plants that accompany us
likewise grow younger, they submit
to reverse evolution.
We've exceeded everything, we return to the past.

Our bodies keep growing younger,
they turn up decimated in other bodies.
Our objects, animals, and plants turn up
in other objects, animals, and plants.
Our planet—in other planets.
Borders—in other borders.
Wars—in other wars.
Our errors, despairs, hopes, loves, wrongs
—in other errors, despairs, hopes, loves, wrongs.

The faster we move into the future, the faster
we return, and nothing,
we can change nothing, save nothing:

we can't save the pyres and the Holy Inquisition
from Giordano Bruno and Jan Hus,
the future from the past,
nothing from oblivion,
oblivion from humanity, and we know
we can't stop now, start over
or even hold still momentarily
without running into

ourselves.

Outskirts

Wars are waged
seasons change
and, so mountain shepherds claim, the climate changes slightly,
which may mean
that we'll survive a new ice age and a new thaw
and be defrosted in better times,
or that we won't survive;
American astronauts circle overhead in "Skylab"
like our dim pangs of conscience,
and are as bored as if they were on earth,
there's not much they can change;
the one-thousand-nine-hundred-seventy-three-year-old
Christ, so often killed and resurrected
in the whole world's prayers,
left the underground, perhaps came down from heaven
and circulates among us like blood in our veins, crosses
streets properly,
his stigmata radiate inhuman light,
but no one sees, they've
got enough trouble with their own nonbeing
and rush to their secular church;
in the evening he's detained by an officer of the law
who's completed marxist-leninist
night school,
true, he has no ID or passport,
and he's never held a job,
but, as he explains, the vision of a better future drew him,

he doesn't need to eat or drink,
since he feeds on light and feels love for people,
which can't possibly justify a show trial
on evidence turned out
by the ardent lathe hands of history;
children-flowers fade slowly in hospitals and on squares
of distant, unknown cities,
every so often someone leaves his car in the street
and tries to find himself,
only to find that he's someone completely different,
which endlessly amazes first-class tourists,
who likewise can't fathom the high tarriffs;
girls, who still walk the streets
as if gently rising above them,
carry notebooks in plastic bags
with printed images of Janis Joplin's face,
Janis Joplin looks just like life, her face
multiplies by the hour,
blood seeps lazily from smashed cars;
in a few hours armies of the Warsaw Pact,
in a few hours the fascist military junta
will transform Chile or some other country
into a giant concentration camp,
profiting from vast experience
in confining entire nations
within a giant prison;
in your little country on planet Phantasmagoria
only women still believe in telepathy,
only women are convinced that yetis do exist,
that we're not alone in the universe,
and that price hikes are at hand;

but even they don't know which prices will rise, maybe
meat as usual or apartments again,
gas or heating oil,
body or blood;
 from the window of your room, as usual,
(if you've got a place to live on planet P.)
you always see the same men,
who've already read the day's papers
announcing the latest price hikes for meat and apartments
in the capitalist world
(today's papers
rot faster than meat and contaminate the air):
someone dropped the Volunteer Reserve Militia ID card
that he sometimes uses to frighten his wife
while casually knocking her up;
women bear their death beneath their hearts,
and only at moments
secretly press their pulsing temples,
and only at moments glance
into the fathomless chasm of shifting clouds,
and only at moments cast unfathomable glances
into the gaudy darkness of the passing moment

into the dazzling gulf of tomorrow's day.

Take a Trip

to Andrzej Urbanowicz

Take a trip—unmoving—that will draw you to the moving world,
a transitory trip that will afix you
in the morning's dazzling white light;

go to the impenetrable darkness: the purest white light without
        beginning or end,
the light that alone endures;

passing the countless stations that were your one permanent address,
forgetting faces of your closest enemies and remotest friends,
forgetting your beloved woman's names—so you'll remember her
        better—
so she won't be just an answer to questions you shouldn't ask

—wounding,
overcoming sleep—death's enchanting intimation,
rejecting the next escape—a small metaphor for the infinity
that lies waiting in every human matter;

take a trip—mortal—that resurrects you,
take a trip to an unknown country, whose capital may be the unknown

and every woman there may bear the blasphemously lovely name of Mary,
don't let serene reflections of dark human matters mislead you,
be guided by a latent, nameless

star

Waxwing, Fly to Heaven

I wake up from a technicolor dream:
kaleidoscopic birds flowers and butterflies
scatter beneath my eyelids

I wake up my eyelids
are pried open by a blunt blade of light
from the barred lamp
burning day and night
in my body's cell
which is not the lamp of my heart or mind

this lamp calmly
lifts its blindness lifts it
to a little heap of rubble bricks
debris and rocks

I wake up from
a good dream to a bad one
through the barred window of my gaze
I see a little heap of rubble
bricks decease and rocks
with a strip of faded newsprint sticking up
I struggle to decipher it:
When the world en

I don't look at the poplars growing by me
in their protective coloration

they're too human in their indifference
all too inhuman as their fate demands
too self-contained

and I don't know if the waxwing
that hops across the rubble seeking food
is the latest incarnation
of what is not yet my I
or if it flew out of my dream
because it saw no other exit
from nonexistence
no other way to know itself

to be someone else

I Believe

to Anna and Stanisław Barańczak

I'll tell the truth: sometimes I believe
in another world's existence, I believe in apparitions,
vampires, sucking brains and blood,
or perhaps it's fear more than belief
(which comes to the same thing these days: fear equals belief).
So I try not to sit with my back to the door,
doors lead their own lives, I'll say more;
I've grown superstitious, I've stopped talking about dreams
and hopes out loud, I'd scare them off, I avoid
pronouncing words that may take vengeance,
I cut them from my old poems (others
do this too), I'll be frank, though,
sometimes I forget to take precautions,
I'll drink vodka, love a woman, leave on a trip, think
telepathically, turn my back
on doors—which lead their own lives
and sooner or later open up,
and sooner or later I'll be touched
by the icy hand that might just give a sign
or may squeeze my heart without warning,
I'll tell the truth; I don't believe this is the hand
of Osip Mandelstam or Georg Trakl
or any other poet who, regardless of the human
or inhuman death that met him,

still speaks to us with his living words.

Insomnia

Insomnia—and wrongs you've done,
wrongs done to you, unrealized
dreams, dreams that can't be realized,

all our daylight, dark and nighttime affairs,
mistakes that can't be avoided, can't be mended

close—imperceptible
distant—indelible

perhaps everything that only death can erase
is like the rain? The Dead Sea

always tossing you to its surface?

*

it's not

that I only have one life
that I might not have been

that I lost faith in distant childhood
that I never stopped being faithful

that I read with shame my recent poems
that I wander through them like embers under snow

that I didn't want to co-falsify
that I don't want to speak half-truths

that nothingness combs through my letters and papers
that it stamps them with its greasy hand

that I scarcely sense what you are

that's not why
I'm learning

silence

A Confession, Not a Poem

I caused dismay when I stopped using
wordplay to amuse—the helpless mimicry
of slaves.

I heard iron laughter
and laughter made of lead. In my larynx
clotted muteness grew. Mute,
I heard mute laughter,

which only now
wounds.

Caute

You open your hand cautiously, it's
blind and dumb. Shameless, stripped bare. Stamped,
entered in the records. Spinoza's friends
are gone now, so are those who denied him,
and the inquisitors of his time,
and the clouds crossing the borders of his time,
and the reasons for his demise likewise no longer obtain;
his coat, quilt, and shirts now
cover no one, new books
are in new bookstores,
exiles in exile, papillary lines
in folders, barbed wire on borders, occupants in apartments,
jurors in boxes, manuscripts in desk drawers, smiles
on lips, blood in veins, workers in workplaces, soldiers
in uniforms, potatoes in stomachs, citizens
in country, documents in pockets, country
inside, foreignness outside, tongue behind teeth, prisoners
in prisons, teeth on concrete, earth in universe
(which either contracts or expands), temperature
in degrees, each in his place, heart
in throat, any questions,

thank you, I see none

Détente

At the very moment that leading animals
from the model agricultural collective
were observing a tour group of distinguished artists,
fraternal clouds
violated the air space
of our new world,
at the very moment that marked the onset of détente
across our entire planet Phantasmagoria,
visual and other artists, working assiduously in time and overtime,
painted over old signboards
and the skin of the old world, taut as Buddha's cheeks,
relaxed; borders of the great powers sought
their place,
southern nations woke up north of midnight
and seemed to sleep-talk in new tongues,

at the moment that everything became possible,
a large transmitter jammed the signals
of lost civilizations,
an ambulance's siren
sliced the city into two incongruent parts,
at the same moment on the sill of my window,
which was just a metaphor,
a raindrop fell
and vanished like an unidentified
flying object
and I vainly sought to tell the surviving crew
what precisely distinguishes our sight,
hearing, touch, taste, and smell

Citizen R. K. Doesn't Live

Citizen R. K. doesn't live
with his wife (or any object
that is his own), he doesn't live by the pen,
by the indigestible fountain pen marked "Parker"
that sticks in his throat: he is a sado-
(he gulps the ink that flows
from the fountain pen marked "Parker")
masochist (with this pen he revives the corpses
of days gone by, so as to harass
them): born (he doesn't
know why): into a worker's family, but just the same
he freeloads (on speech): an honorary
blood donor (does foreign blood flow
in his veins): against our
death penalty: he tried to smuggle
something across the border: a birth
certificate, his collective
organism, and a fountain pen ("Parker"): he
doesn't jot down thoughts, he communicates tele-
pathically (there's a snake
in his telephone) and he corrupts underaged
wristwatches: to fall asleep he counts to 19
84 (isn't he counting on nothing?). He lives,
though it remains unclear

whether he deserves such a life

Still Seeking

Where do you hurry, my heart,

as if still seeking
your incarnation?

Like a Dream

Truly, your life is like a dream,
a train trip, a stroll down a surviving avenue;

it continues imperceptibly, alters invisibly:

it drags on—and—crisscrossing
itself only by known roads—

relentlessly delivers you
to bygone afternoons

or generations.

Blow

"The blow fell from the most unlikely corner . . ."

So might begin the account
of life's origins on earth

or any other irreversible event

Sometimes When You Say

Sometimes when you say: it's not too late yet,
it's not time yet,
nothing has happened yet
that requires your response

your *nothing* doesn't rest
and doesn't exist in secret—but is, is
a relentless killer,
it doubles and triples
so as best to discharge its shifting duties
and though its strengths cannot be exhausted

—it sees no end to its task.

Who'd Understand

Who'd understand your sense of equality better
than your pedigreed dog?

About Time

He turns back more than once to see
if he's really locked the front door:

it's about time
that windows and doors, taps, faucets, and pesky gas valves
began producing affidavits—

to say nothing
of the electric irons that suddenly
come to mind in trains.

"O"

Optimism grows from day to day:

from day to day its "O" expands;
in opposition to its "O," its "p"
(which opens pessimism)
doesn't alter its dimensions
(it objectively remains itself,
while subjectively submitting to reduction)

O, you're running short on other words

you converse with "O,"
you voyeurize with "O,"
you eavesdrop with "O,"
you soothe intimate needs with "O,"
you nod off with a great "O" on your lips
and wake up with an even greater one:
you grow ever more open,
your lips open ever wider,
not to shriek, not to smile,
not to please, not to be believed;

it defies belief: you wake up with a letter,
a number? a vowel? on your lips,
a growing "O,"

that doesn't see a world outside itself

No Need

No need to search,
they turn up on their own, slaves,
ready to yield the power
that only

love and fatal illness
hold over us.

TRANSLATED WITH STANISŁAW BARAŃCZAK

You Receive Letters

You receive letters with stamps
on which your country ripples
like a banner in the wind;

the letter's white shadow spreads and folds its arms,
the letter's white dove spreads and folds its wings,
and the wind flapping flags
and the wind wrapped in flags
behaves in keeping with its nature.

Wastepaper, Scrap

Atlantologists of the future,

our little victories and great defeats,
our little truths and great lies,
our concrete cities,
our incurable diseases,
our radioactive dust,
our minor hopes and great illusions

did in fact exist.

Those calcified strata
are our bones.

Those imperishable plastic objects
were not our talismans, we used them
for daily purposes.

The glass cubes
were not our deities, although they were employed
in efforts
to bend our will
and break our characters.

It sometimes happened
that even our thoughts were overheard.

True,
we multiplied in bestial fashion
and consumed our brothers: animals and plants,
in order to sustain our own
species.

We should not have killed one another
in the name of an inhuman Chimera:
a better future.

Atlantologists of a future time,
wastepaper, scrap,
if they endure
may not be our best witness

—and we knew that we existed.

Our Life Grows

Our life grows like fear and panic,
our life grows like bread lines;

our life grows like grass, like dust and like moss,
like a spiderweb, frost, and a colony of mold;
our life grows relentlessly like coughs and laughter,
in spite of wars, treaties, and negotiations,
détentes, climate changes, the UN,
tacit exploitation and open tyranny,
the pomp of black limousines and soulless judges,
secreting services, subordinate nonentities,
polluting newspapers and transplanted hearts,
covert diplomacy and open lies,
mockery of sacred truths,
poisoned air and quaking earth;

our life grows uncontrollably, on smoking ruins
and in deepest sleep,
above us, around and through us, who are
its prodigal sons,
our life grows, like hidden price hikes, science fiction,
like blood pressure, fictitious empires,
fear of being late to work or looking straight into the eye;

our life grows like a fetus, like famine,
our life grows like flora and fauna,
but our life doesn't grow like hate, thirst for vengeance,

or hunger for retaliation
and even when it doesn't know what it wants,
our life wants to live

like a human.

You Are

You are my only homeland.

You are my only homeland, silence,
which holds all
the futile words;

mute clouds,
breaths, glances,
carrier pigeon with a letter
gone without a trace;

you are my homeland, stillness,
shrieking in
dead tongues;

like the victim of a fire,
who's lost everything useless,
like the fugitive
caught just outside the camp

though I'm not your child
or your prisoner,
I know that even in exile
I'll remain inside you, speech,
and you'll be in me
like a swollen tongue: heart
keeping me alive

until it won't

What Luck

What luck: two survivors from Warsaw,
Bethar, the Drohobycz ghetto,
we meet in a main station
built on ashes, breaths, and dust of the dead,
murdered, nameless, lost without a trace,
and we silently recall our dead,
murdered, nameless causes, lost without a trace,
deathless heaven and dead landscapes,
liberty, equality, fraternity, sympathy,
the alpha and omega of smoke buried shallowly in the resettled air,
strips of scorched paper, apparitions of books and letters
lifted by currents rising ever farther and higher,
crossing all inhuman, mobile and murderous borders,
the shadows of burnt books, scattering at a touch,
the phantoms of our old and new, dead and living tormenters;
and we remember our old teachers
and the girls now living only in our hearts
along with the ceaseless clatter of their shoes

beyond spectral windows.

Much Easier

Your heart transmits and receives signals
from lost civilizations

your brain is a dead city in the distant future
grave robbers raise new mausoleums

papillary lines revolve in unknown spaces
card files have been burnt or pulped

your "you" is startled by your "I"

"nothing's for certain" took the elevator down
while "anything can happen"
climbed the stairs

you grow harder harder
it's much easier than it seems

Calmly and Quietly

to Jan Lebenstein

Our fear is premature: incurable diseases,
earthquakes, urgent trips,
belated telegrams—and eyes glued
to our nape

but this all comes at its own pace,
without haste—and without delay,
precisely when its hour strikes,

not always in its final shape right off,

calmly and quietly, leaving no trace in the sandy
landscape

like the hour of a train's departure
or going to a movie.

Issa

to Danusia and Adam

Issa, of whom I read not long ago
that he knew poverty and want
but lived happily to old age,
says in one of his untranslatable poems:
"Climb, little snail,
up Mount Fuji,
but slowly." Slowly.

Don't hurry, words and heart.

There Are

There are concealed world wars,
imperceptible infections of the lungs and hearts under attack.

Maybe It's You

At last we're on equal terms; I'm
always pressed for time. I go to work
in debt, on a crowded tram
maybe it's you who hates (some sort of)

me with all your might.

TRANSLATED WITH STANISŁAW BARAŃCZAK

I'll Remember That

Remember
I'm your friend:

you can tell me everything.

And you can tell me everything too.

I'll remember that,
oh stone.

TRANSLATED WITH STANISŁAW BARAŃCZAK

Rose

Open secret, simple labyrinth,

careless, deathless,
foreboding rose, I still don't want,

I still don't have the right to die.

TRANSLATED WITH STANISŁAW BARAŃCZAK

My Little Girl Learns to Read

My little girl, infallible till now,
learns to read and write
and makes mistakes for the first time

and I live through my old errors
of humankind once more

TRANSLATED WITH STANISŁAW BARAŃCZAK

Inscription on a Piece of China

I am like this dish: you can only accept me,
do not try to alter
or repair.

TRANSLATED WITH STANISŁAW BARAŃCZAK

You, Moment

You, moment, you were my sweetheart,
I held you, flying, in my failing arms,
I embodied you,
became a living anchor
when at the dim dawn
my pulse beat inside you
repeating syllables from an ancient source

and only mute doors
choked with sobs

In Spherical Sleep

She runs, flees
in spherical
sleep.

She's alone.
Who will hear
if she whispers for help?

Pain wakes her.
She's alone. Only he
now shares life

with her.

My Beloved

My beloved, moments ago
you still walked in your favorite black dress
beneath a sun projecting
shadows of shifting triangles
(intelligible even to me, who
never understood geometry):

the distance grows, draws close,
a relentless straight line
penetrates my heart,
between us lies not even the smoke
of a train departing years ago

but this intimate remoteness
in labyrinths of seals, stamps,
coiled wire and borders

weaves its barbed net

PARIS, SEPTEMBER 1977

93

Books, Paintings

Books, paintings, an amber necklace,
an apartment, if we live that long,
pupil of the sky's eye and a dewdrop,
tiger shell, passport, memory,
human homeland without armies or borders,
wedding rings, photos, manuscripts,
five liters of blood (together: ten), hunger,
dusks and the gift of morning,

we can lose everything,
everything can be taken from us

except the independent,
nameless words,
even if they only flow through us,
except the sacred word, which even
when written in dead languages of ice

will see resurrection

Buddha, Christ

Buddha, Christ

in vain you hide
inside so many incarnations

But Above All

I pray
with meager words
that hunger, handicaps, unearned
illnesses and sufferings should cease;

but above all,
Almighty Beginning,
You who burdened us with freedom,
leaving us to resolve
all our human and inhuman affairs alone,

oh Almighty
Whose Name
I dare not speak,

rather slay me
before I'm ever
forced to kill
in any faith's name,

take my speech
before I'm ever tempted
in any truth's name

to exalt myself

(It, Sleepless

It was I,
though sick and hungry myself,
who deserted the house,
as sickness and hunger held sway there.

I am: not. Mute,
long forgotten,
it circles the unpeopled streets.

Night, one of many, the only.

In someone's dark window
lashed by the moon's cold light
a shadow dims).

Hangs
on a cross.

(Forgive me.
And You forgive me, and You.)

VIENNA, NOVEMBER 1977

Almost All

It's the twentieth century,
I take the newspaper to bed,
glasses, pills and wristwatch
in arm's reach:
I don't know if I'll sleep,
I don't know if I'll wake

that's all.

TRANSLATED WITH STANISŁAW BARAŃCZAK

Pass It On

Independent nonentities, let's transmit
the clouds' skyscraping script,

we'll keep passing it from mouth to mouth.

Who Isn't

Fear the God
who isn't

in your heart.

Let Us Pray

for the living the dead
for the unbegotten and unborn
for fratricides and suicides
for slaves
and for victims of force,
for the exalted and for the abased,
for the poor and for the destitute,
for the forgotten and for those
whom we do not wish to remember.

Let us pray
for a human death.

For an end to the death penalty.

Let us not pray for triumph,
let us pray to endure.

We dare to pray

for Your watchful gaze

We ask You;
be,

heed us

and hear us out

Do Not Want to Die for Us

Do not want to die for us,
do not want to live for us:

live with us.

TRANSLATED WITH STANISŁAW BARAŃCZAK

Not Much

Our poor dead
gaze at us with their
empty eyes
and see everything to come—
but even they can't help

or warn us,

since neither war nor peace

has taught us much.

Sleep Well

Sleep well,
the devil keeps watch:
he eavesdrops and spies
on our most secret fears and dreams
so as to learn something new

from us too.

TRANSLATED WITH STANISŁAW BARAŃCZAK

Borne on the Wind

The wind bears scraps
of an indecipherable sheet of paper:
forgotten words? a dream?
my mute you?

trembles on my tongue's tip.

Unseen

Unseen eyes
see with my eyes,
an unseen heart

has me in hand.

So What

So what if you can be human
if you love equally

your own and others' children;

so what if you can be masculine, feminine,
and female,
so what if you can't manage on your own;

so what if you are the one and only,
all-embracing, righteous
homeland,
since we have to die for you;

so what if sometimes nothing revives us
like you,

so you're immortal,

so what,

death.

I Can't Help You

Poor moth, I can't help you,
I can only turn out the light.

TRANSLATED WITH STANISŁAW BARAŃCZAK

You've Climbed High

You've climbed high, my little snail,
to the black lilac's highest leaf!

But remember: September's nearly over.

WEST BERLIN, SEPTEMBER 1979

Rights

—What rights
do you mean?
The right to life?
You can't extend it even by an instant,
though you're dying of curiosity:
who won, who killed.
—The right to fight?
The right of the fittest comes first ...
—So you're speaking not of human
rights,
but laws of nature,
just try to win this argument with her:

may your triumph

not defeat you.

Must You Really

Must you really be made of stone
to know how to live

and die?

Go to Sleep

Fear, go to sleep. Don't sleep.
If all else fails, then

sleep with open eyes.

Yes, She Says

Yes, she says, I survived.
Now I face an equally
grave task: to get
on a tram,

to get home.

TRANSLATED WITH STANISŁAW BARAŃCZAK

You're All Free

You're all free—says the guard
and the iron gate shuts

this time from the other side.

TRANSLATED WITH STANISŁAW BARAŃCZAK

Who Knows

If all of us together
in all our languages
yelled "Help!" at the same instant
then who knows, maybe light years later
the indestructible jamming stations
of our other world
might detect an answer

like an echo.

We Can Destroy

We can destroy
all our evidence and still
even the mute rings of trees,
even our mute bones will tell

what times we lived in.

I Didn't Know

Going to school
each day I saw
the Prussian barracks towering
above the city: I didn't know
that the poet Gottfried Benn
had worked there as an army doctor in the war.
I didn't know much back then about illness

or poetry.

A Stop

During an endless stop
in East Berlin
a young customs officer zealously unscrews
the tin ceiling
in the car's corridor; standing on tiptoe,
he checks for fugitives; his uniform shirt
creeps up to reveal a plump,
helpless tummy cradling

a holster.

TRANSLATED WITH STANISŁAW BARAŃCZAK

Realism

The dove of peace's ghost,
a little white flag in its beak,
flies above the Berlin Wall:
a sniper
keeps it in his sights.

TRANSLATED WITH STANISŁAW BARAŃCZAK

Read: Homeland

Zebrzydowice Station
(read: homeland).

Why are you rifling
through my books,
though they're written in Polish,
the language will be strange to you:
the departure sticks tight
to the return
like two sides of the same
sheet scrawled in childish ciphers;

a plate of bullet proof glass,
it shields me from the world before morning,
and from bygone cities, glances, birds in flight,
it summons shadows known only

to itself.

Stronger Than Fear

What is poetry which does not save
nations or people?
  −Czesław Miłosz

What is poetry, what can it save?
Only the names, the shadows
of people and things?

What else could it be, except a voice anxious
as a human heartbeat,
stronger than the fear of poverty and death,
a voice

of conscience that neither nations nor people,
brutal wars, pogroms,
can kill

or conquer?

New Day

The Veterans' Cooperative "Twenty Years of People's Poland"
waits for its new office, the wind blows,
Holocene sands grind, hair falls out.
Your unemployed you
passes by a line that grows before your eyes behind a newsstand.
A crumpled newspaper
with a photo, already fading, of the new leader
takes flight and falls beneath an ambulance's
wheels. Open,
open the telegram tied in pink ribbon,
maybe the cobalt helped.
When you take your child to preschool
in a postwar barrack, you'll see, as you do every day,
a guard on the wall
who never takes his eyes

from what's happening on the other side.

TRANSLATED WITH STANISŁAW BARAŃCZAK

*

Lapse? Absentmindedness? Accident?
A little lizard, flickering through thorns and ivy,
led me to you on an island of the dead
enclosed by walls of azure and water.
I still admire your small poems
but I can't understand your life.
Oh well, Ezra. I don't know much. I've got to get back. The pebble
I'd like to take from the path for remembrance
looks deep inside, shuts tight, stays mute.
I leave it to the earth and no one's silence.

Almost Like

No, not a dream: almost like
a street in a strange town
that you'll never see now,
you recall words and addresses,
so few remain:
deaf telephone, deaf snow,
a crowbar's traces on the door—
what can be saved?
Two sentences, the house's number,
don't waste them, keep them
for a black hour.
Go, don't look back.

Proceed with both eyes open.

Facing the Wall

A woman turns the mirror

to face the wall: now the wall
reflects the dead snow
crunching under iron soles.
The fire freezes.
Nothingness affixes bayonets.

DECEMBER 1981

TRANSLATED WITH STANISŁAW BARAŃCZAK

*

I don't know if I have the right
to speak, keep still, touch
wounds. I pray. No
words. He

Knows.

Just Passing

Two turtledoves on a leafless tree:

if you're just passing
hurt and hungry through pigeon Warsaw,
you'll find your own way to my Master,

Mr. Cogito,
Prince of Poets.

How Could I

What are you doing, little snail, on my balcony,
so many floors above the ground!
Are you coming back from Fuji?
Oh, how could I

not know you, Issa, at once?

The Age

The age of progress liberated demons
of which the Middle Ages
never dreamed....

Gladly

The masters of the Last Judgment
painted hell more gladly
than purgatory

Purgatorium

Night, an empty compartment. I want
nothing, fear no one. Glowing in the distance,
the little flames of purgatory: my city.

Nothing, Night

Nothing, night beyond the glass
looks through me with the nongaze
of the boy I was, am

not, won't be.

I Forgot

I tried to teach my dog patience.
My God, I forgot,
you gave him a different life.

Answered

I sighed:
and was answered by the deep sigh
of my dog.

This Country

In this country? Yes, I stayed in this country.
Exile comes in many shapes

and places.

At Least

A misprint, a lapsus linguae
may change the course of history
—or at least of poetry.

How to Write?

To write so that a hungry man
might think it's bread?

First feed the hungry man,
then write so that his hunger
won't go in vain.

*

So you want to exist, little line?
If you would sow despair, cause pain,

begone, foul fiend.

Who Finds Comfort

To flee with your soul on a leaf ...
–Adam Mickiewicz

Who finds comfort
in a sentence made of metal?
I'd rather read on a little leaf
a poem by the snail Issa,
who once before, after centuries,
brought me urgent news

from a free world.

Almost Haiku

> *An invisible crow circles overhead*
> *do you see it?*
> —Hans Arp

A crow's cuneiform on the snow:
I'm not extinct.
You who read this

aren't either.

*

Blind? Deaf? Mute?
Incomprehensible?

It is. It aches.

Vortex

—Thanks for coming. I was
sick, frightened
by words and people. Already ...

—There's not much time. Friends in purgatory
said to warn you. Don't sleep at home
tomorrow night. Again ...

you're torn in two directions by
a vortex of dawn
and dreams.

From a Travel Diary of 1985

I crossed the border
with childish ease. Neither guards
nor customs caught my simple trick.

My astonished friends
ask gaily: how did I
do it. I was just about to find out myself

when the milkman rang the bell.

Auden, Lines

to Staszek, with thanks
for the Collected Poems

Wystan Hugh Auden: I didn't know
languages. While packing
I misplaced the famous photo
with its cosmic map of wrinkles leading
farther than earth's lines of fate,
of the heart and head.

It's only now been given me to read
—and I don't want much: to translate
"Marginalia,"
"A Thanksgiving"—if
my life line doesn't
mislead me?—or maybe it's the line

of luck?

Crossed-out Opening

for Zbigniew Herbert

A crossed-out opening, on the other
side: white,

between them so much life, in-
describable—

—still a sheet of paper; crumpled
in the ashtray it burns,

a little infinity? nothing?
a touch of light and shadow

*

This year
I bore no fruit,

just leaves
that leave no shadows

I am afraid, Rabbi,

I am afraid, Lord,

that I'll be cursed by him who hungers,

weary
on the endless road
to Jerusalem

*

so was it worth it to bring down holy speech
  –Zbigniew Herbert (tr. Alissa Valles)

I've known more good than evil—
for help I was given
weak hands and sight,
a relatively clear head,
the genes of life, fear,
a time to harm, a time to repent:

a sinful tongue
that I no longer wish to use

holy speech,
of which
I feel unworthy

MARCH 1987

147

*

Blind? Deaf? Mute?
Incomprehensible?

It is.

Silence

His terrifying fits of rage

*

He worked hard in the forest, he knew how to do everything. He wanted to teach me everything too, since he believed that only physical labor would save me when the next war came. Remember, they'll know you by your hands, he used to say. If your hands are rough, you go right, if they're delicate, educated, you go left, to the camps or up against a wall.

He taught me to plow, to use a scythe, to reap. To tell edible from inedible plants. Most are edible, you won't starve to death—he said. He tried teaching me to fish, but quickly gave up; I proved to be a remarkably stubborn pupil. He showed me how to build a hut, to dig a shelter. Even how to make a fire, though he'd never managed it himself.

He taught me to use an ax. I was a little boy, but I could chop wood as well as my virtual comrade in misery from *The Seven Samurai*. And also from *The Magnificent Seven*? I don't remember.

More than anything, though, for reasons I still don't understand, he wanted me to learn to swim and to stay under water as long as I could. It may save your life when you have to escape—he'd repeat.

During my next-to-last summer vacation, we worked together in the woods. He gave me the easiest job, wood barking. We'd leave in the morning, get back at night. On the way home he liked to take dips in a woodland lake. One evening he dived in as usual and didn't come back up. I thought he'd swum across and was waiting for me on the other side. I circled the lake, not a trace. His stuff had vanished too.

I went around a second time, a third, no luck. I didn't know what to do. Scared, I couldn't find the road in the dark. I wandered a long time before I got home.

He was there, as if nothing had happened. Alone. Mother had gone out looking for me in the night. He was silent. So was I. I was afraid to say anything.

And that's how it stayed.

I didn't learn much. I would have died in the wilderness. I would have died trying to escape.

*

When the telegram came, I went straight to the hospital from the station. He lay in an oxygen tent. He wasn't expecting me, he gazed at me absently. At last he recognized me. He cried. His right lung, removed a few days earlier, already journeyed through its uncertain, crippled afterlife.

The Face

It gave me no peace through my entire childhood, spent in my parents' house, which had been abandoned by its German occupants, with the blue inscription in tiles — *Sich regen bringt Segen* — lording over the kitchen stove; even my miraculously restored father couldn't translate this for me. A face. A grotesquely (I wouldn't learn this word for some time yet) twisted face in the wood circles on the upper left-hand corner of the door separating the room I slept in from the kitchen.

Not my entire childhood, of course. I first noticed it the day my father went out walking for a few hours and came back from the nearest town with a terrible headache. On the threshhold, my poor mother tried to undo the spells that someone (some village woman, she said, since it couldn't be a wolf, a dog, a viper, a frog or any kind of bird) must have cast on him. First she tossed hot coals into a pan of cold water, but she'd barely got them all counted, in the negative — not one, not two, and so on up to nine — before they sank. This boded no good.

From then on, the face stubbornly fixed its eyes on me, its gaze followed me. I hid in the farthest corner and looked out the window for hours. Once it became the face of a strange man who appeared from nowhere and jabbered for ages in his convoluted, ancient wooden speech, which I couldn't remember when I woke up, not a single word or sound.

Screams frightened me. I was even more afraid of laughter. I had no one to tell. As soon as I'd finished school, I set off for the city. I embraced the art of escape, the Kunst der Fuge in a bounded space. I studied the art of memory and the art of forgetting. But years later, as my father lay dying of cancer in that same room, he told me deliriously—I've tried painting over that face so many times, it still stares at me.

A Stone from the Village of New World

As soon as I turned it over, I saw that the heavy sandstone circle, which looked like the top part of a quern, a grindstone, or a well cover, had been carved from an old Jewish tombstone. The mutilated inscription showed only the dead woman's name, [Br]ejnche (Bräunche?), that she'd been widowed, and the date of her death: *at night on the fourth day of the eight day of the month elul 595* (or *598?*) *according to the minor order of counting*—that is, either September 2, 1835, or August 29, 1838, if I've calculated correctly. The exact date can't be made out, since a square hole was cut in the middle of the circle that once held the key letter.

I found the stone in a yard overgrown with weeds and bushes, just after buying a run-down house in the hamlet of New World: I'd picked it more for the auspicious name than for the place itself. Exiles like me—from the East, from beyond the Bug River— settled here after the war. Germans had lived here before, they left a moldy scrap of a 1936 newspaper in the attic and countless broken medicine bottles.

I'm not asking when and how it ended up here, or who committed this atrocity. I only want to preserve it from further destruction, I seek a refuge more lasting than my weak letters. I don't know what to do. What wall should hold it? Nothing remains of the nearest Jewish cemetery (in a place once called Brodziec, then Brätz, and now something else)—this must be where it came from—nor can anyone tell me where the cemetery was. I don't know what I am or am not permitted to do with it. I don't even know if I'm permitted to guard the gravestone for the moment. I don't know whose advice to ask, or how much time I've got.

Fragments from 1989

. . . . .

mute,
with covered head,
I stand with a pebble in my mouth
before a wall of fire
and forgetting

counted
among the helpers
of death

. . . .

take the ashes from me,
take the weight of not
my fault, let me bear
to the other shore

the wounds: remorse,

regret

. . . .

dawn, the color of the Seine,
the color of wormwood and bile

. . . .

your body already no one's
floating from nowhere to nowhere

. . . .

the maimed world dawns

City

Above all it prizes order, cleanliness, and thrift:
the synagogue became a public pool,
the market parking lots betray
no trace of Jewish graves.

*

Others

may close, but this one, impalpable,
painfully exposed,
keeping you from living—and still
keeping you alive, this one only, forever
unhealed, for you
alone, may it remain

open

I Was Here

A flash, a ray's fading hieroglyph on the wall—
a helpless spell, repeated stubbornly,
"Kilroy was here," like the lichen's
etchings. In a niche of dusk a homeless man
unfolds his cartons for the night. No one

is reflected on the wall.

Someone, Kaspar Hauser

Someone, Kaspar Hauser?
Not this time, someone like other of my
stillborn I's, mute Minotaur,
seen in dreams, the dream last
night, his stony wanderings
through labyrinths of subways, fold

the bandages and cinders

1991

*

My crazy dog is long gone now.
We shared this too, I think, feeling
the tension grow inside me
as I draw close to places where I once
came to grief.

*

"To love and betray, to yearn and curse ... "
Who wrote that? Not I? I, he? I, it?
I, no one?

Dawn, grief, and guilt.
Oh wife, wife.

A Quarter to Midnight

Your voice in the receiver
is covered by another voice that I
don't even try to understand. Maybe it's calling 911,
telling an answering machine "I
love you," dumping stocks, cursing,
sobbing. Out of the ozonosphere? From the Atlantic's
floor? A quarter to midnight

of no one's time.

Rue de Poitiers

Late afternoon, light snow.
The Musée d'Orsay's on strike, nearby
a gray lump bundled on the sidewalk's edge:
a bum curled in a ball (maybe a refugee
from some country caught in civil war)
still lying on the grate, packed in a quilt,
a scrap-heap sleeping bag, the right to life.
Yesterday his radio was playing.
Today coins cooling on a paper shape constellations,

nonexistent moons and planets.

NOVEMBER 1995

The Angel Ikrzak

So you still live and paint your magic pictures
on ever smaller cardboard squares. I'll visit you
more often, if I may. Yes of course,
I remember, just knock twice on a wall

made of weariness and mist.

*

No *Carceri d'Invenzione*, no light in the tunnel:
still, seven minutes spent wandering through charred darknesses,
along walls of a corridor, all right angles,
and I know even less how I'll ever slip unseen

through the nearest eternity

Among Them, in Their Midst

Twelve men at a table laid for fates: they know that one will be a
traitor and another will deny three times before the cock crows once
(or twice, accounts remain unclear). With them, among them, in the
very midst of his infinite singularity, the master, teacher. He who
is proof against numbers. Son of the unmentionable Name. Son of
man. He has just finished breaking the matzoh, for the very last time,
he lifts a glass of wine. His face is hidden from us. His hair, sprinkled
with spikenard, emanates unearthly light. His few words reach us in
variants and translations. Careful, endlessly amended, after so many
wars, how faithful can they be.

Frost

A whisper's gray frost, fossilized despair. Who will catch
the earth's fading psalm, the mute greetings between
planets, the galaxies' farewells. Black suns
collapse into themselves
in inhuman

silence.

Whatever

I don't do everything from love for you.
I love you

whatever I do.

Silent, Soaring

Silent, soaring,
early autumn light
glowed past the window.

I miss you.

Take Me

Take me to your sleep.
Let me stay there.
Let me spin
until I melt

beneath your lids.

Copenhagen

Oh yes, I was even in Copenhagen.
One leg only, true enough.
En route from London to Warsaw?
Waiting for my plane
I stood before a vast pane of glass
in the departure hall
and gazed at an opaque city
more inscrutable
than what was still not long ago

the dark side of the moon.

Gingko

Single being, doubled in myself,
I planted a Japanese gingko
(in Goethe's honor
of course).

I didn't want it to be lonely.
But to see if it was male or female
I'd need to keep living
for at least another forty years.

Not likely.

If my poem survives,
plant a companion,
female, male,
for the duration.

For gingkos
the slight gap in age
will make no difference.

What There?

I wake at 3:16.
In my dream it was exactly three past four,
I saw that clearly on a church clock
in London? Budapest?

A moment earlier I'd talked about Brecht,
with György Petri,
just my age,
who died two years ago.

(Truth be told, we were silent,
although we knew exactly what we meant).

So fine—I broke in—but tell me,
what's it like there?

What there—he shrugged—
when we're both here.

The Museum of Fine Arts in Budapest

How did you end up here,
Egyptian princess's poor mummy,
on display for strangers' eyes?
This is your afterlife now.
I'm in it for the moment
that I look at you.

It's the only afterlife so far.
No one knows
if others follow.

Secretly

Secretly, discreetly
I lift my older brother,
the snail,
from the path,
so that no one will step on him.

Older by a million years or so.
Brother in uncertain existence.
Both alike not knowing
what we were created for.
Both alike writing mute questions,
each in his most intimate script:

frightened sweat, sperm, mucus.

In Basel , Nearly Twenty-Six Years Later

Only for a few hours then, en route from Paris to Vienna.
In the old Burberry raincoat of Zygmunt Hertz, an emigrant.

This time in my own coat, from a newer generation,

though no less frayed.

MAY 2003

Leaving Assisi

Crippled Giotto. Loudly: Silenzio!
From a truck passed on the road
transporting animals
I'm caught by the helpless
gaze of a calf
taken to slaughter.

Help me, Saint Francis.
Appear at the abattoir gates.
And if you're otherwise engaged,
then send
your brother Sylvester

or the wolf of Gubbio.

Munich Airport, Transit

Stairs, moving sidewalks, Europe, stairs.
Watch for unattended luggage.
Front page headline:
"Hauptgewinn: Ein Baby."

A different world, business, behind the curtain now—
until we land, though,
our chances of success (no stroke, no heart attack,
and so on)
are
equal in this world.

"First Prize: Baby."
Teenaged Jessica
from New York
has had her five minutes
for several weeks now:
on TV she plays,
in her words,
"God's part,
as they say."

(She hosts a quiz show
to select the lucky parents
who'll receive her soon-to-be-born
child).

Newspapers: stubborn shuffling of free newspapers
included in the fare.

Pinakothek: the Old, the New, now the Contemporary too,
the Dionysus of Exekias, of Zbigniew Herbert,
the male cat (or female too?) from a seemingly simple poem
Meeting with a Different Species

(I translated it for a long time,
almost a neon minute—
that perhaps continues
on the Geiger counter of the Ineffable,
whose part in the States
is played by Jessica?),

the earth, sweet concrete underfoot.

Below. Beneath the clouds' snowy cover.
Uncertain. Out of reach.

MAY 3, 2004

Cologne, Distant

Landing in Cologne,
which I won't see this time,
I repeat the poem to myself:
Köln, Am Hof.

I translated it under Martial Law.
I thought "Am Hof" was a hotel.
No way to check.
Cologne was distant
(and besides I had no passport).

Only much later, while revising
Independent Nonentities,
at a friend's house outside Warsaw
I found on a borrowed map
the little street
at the foot
of a vast cathedral.

Paul Celan
once stopped there,
poet, exile, Jew,
neighbor.

Waking Up

Bonn? Is it really Bonn?
I dreamed of the street in Freiburg
lined with gingkos,
and W. G. Sebald
(*I sense it. Vertigo.*)

We read on the same day,
but not a word passed between us,
and I'm sorry.

MAY 4, 2004

The Effect of Foreignness

I'd rather read my poems in a foreign language:
the sharp pebbles of correct pronunciation
that tumble in my mouth help

keep me from feeling my confession's shame.

Sweet, Innocent

Sweet, innocent words,
sweet, full sentences,
from sweet, gently
curving commas
seep pure

poison

NOWY ŚWIAT, JULY 8, 2004, B.

Joseph Brodsky's Grave

Where the greasy sea
licks the gates.

In the evangelical section
near Ezra Pound
and Olga Rudge.

Faithful guests vanish:
an aggressive gull,
timid lizards.

At the base,
beneath a guttered votive,
someone has placed
(in a plastic sleeve
to keep out rain)
a computer print-out photo:

Brodsky, ill, gaunt,
in front of the four tetrarchs.

Whole in his
intent gaze.
On the grave, oblations:

an upturned tumbler with small coins,
an empty vodka bottle

with a faded label,
twists of paper
tucked into the greenery
(poems maybe? letters?
petitions? curses?)

A plastic bucket
full of ballpoints

(enough for another,
far longer life).

Black plastic glasses

(plastic again,
the mark of time).

Pebbles on the gravestone,
as on a macewa, a Jewish tomb,

a pinecone, a little leaf.

In Berlin

In Berlin, once West,
before a bookshop window
I recall a girl
from a poem by Jürgen Fuchs,
a friend, a poet
followed by the Stasi
even here,
on the free side
of the wall.

I translated it
some twenty years ago.
Many of you
hadn't yet been born.

Jürgen
was still alive then.

He was younger than I.

We saw each other rarely,
usually in passing,
usually by accident.

On the other side,
if we meet by chance,
it will likely be the same.

If it is.

Chestnut

While I stood at the grave of Doctor Franz Kafka
in the New Jewish Cemetery in Prague
the last chestnut fell
from a nearby chestnut tree
and glowed for a moment
in the afternoon light of late fall
among other chestnuts,
leaves, letters,

pebbles and stones.

Pigeons

In the poem *Last words*
written just before his death,
Zbigniew Herbert recalls
the poet Miroslav Holub

who while feeding pigeons
from a seventh-story window
fell out

A Czech typo?

Since I read in the paper
that it was Bohumil Hrabal
who fell from a hospital window
while feeding pigeons.

(Which turned out to be
a lovely legend
dreamed up by the media).

I don't know if Herbert
read Hrabal.
I don't know
if Holub, that gentle surrealist,
(I met him once in Mälmo)
liked pigeons.

But I remember Herbert
feeding a turtledove
on the kitchen windowsill
of his apartment
near the Promenade
in February, 1982.

(It was still harsh winter
and Martial Law.)

Herbert. Holub. Hrabal.

Three different fates.
Three gray pigeons
and yet another

owl's riddle.

*

Through exhaust fumes comes the scent of rotting apples
full of acrid melancholy and heavy metals.
If Friedrich Schiller were walking here, not me,
he might compose new xenias (or an elegy)—
but even fortune's darling, the Muses' favorite,
privy councillor Goethe

entertains elsewhere today.

Folk Etymology

I was born in Austria during the war
so my village schoolmates *from Poland* called me: Kangaroo.
But usually for them I was Russky, Kraut, Jew.

Captain Nemo

Does anyone else still know the word *bezodnia*, pond?
Captain No One, beneath a shallow pond, two years after Stalin's death,
I dreamed of sailing underseas for twenty thousand leagues.

Esprit de l'escalier
or a Belated Answer to a Certain Question

Alas, I have delayed reflexes.
That's why I like tall stairways.
That's why I occasionally write.

After Rain

Brother and sister, enigmatic sphinx, noble snail:
what fate does your shaky script record
on the runway, in a lethal century's last autumn?

OCTOBER 2000

So

Goldfinches, skylarks, turtledoves, nightingales.
So creation preferred dinosaurs
in their later incarnation?

Truth?

What is the truth?
Where are its headquarters?
Where is its board of directors?
Where is its legal team?
Where are its bodyguards?
Where is its PR division?
Where is its marketing?
Who are its overseers?
Who handles follow-up?
Who are its media sponsors?
How does it sell?
Has it gone public?

What are its shares going for?

Might Have

"When you die, you'll be ... "

If not for a wrong number from another hemisphere
that woke me in the middle of the night,
I might have learned

at last.

DECEMBER 23, 2002

To Touch

"To touch the heart of things."
I dreamed once
that I touched the heart of things.
Blindly, from inside

a stone.

Frail Manuscripts

The old poet's frail manuscripts
bear traces of ash, countless cigarette
holes, coffee stains, less often,
red wine, and now and then
the almost unintelligible prints
of cat paws, vanishing

into spacetime.

2001

Cats

The Lord God got cats right—
Wisława Szymborska sometimes says.
Sometimes she adds: Only.
Sometimes: The best.

How Many Worlds

How many more worlds, how many antiworlds,
apparent worlds, reflected worlds,
erupted worlds, ingested worlds

how many other worlds

flare then fade,
fade then flare

in a grain of sand,
in a stone's eye
on a perished planet
revolving, ever swifter,
around a white,
then black dwarf,
along the rim of
one of maybe
a hundred twenty five
billion

vanishing galaxies

As Always, Different

First I have to call up childhood's threshold,
to set the course. East straight ahead,
the right hand's south, north to the left, the rest behind
my back. As always, different
from where I think.

"You just have to imagine doors"

A sudden downpour washed away
my high school records. Who am I? When? My
beloved teacher, Herr Professor Bruno Schulz,
spreads his hands helplessly: "Try at least
to carve a boat from bark!"

from Haiku from Last Winter

* * * *

Greetings, my sparrow!
I see that we've both survived
this frostbitten night.

* * * *

Peacock butterfly?!
Frail beauty in a mourning
cloak of folded wings.

* * * *

A million haiku!
But how many will outlast
Basho's hopping frog?

* * * *

And more cranes fly past!
Today feels like spring, but what
about tomorrow?

* * * *

The snow's nearly gone.
Sorrow, it may be time for you
to get going too.

* * * *

Ladybug waiting
on the door! Where have you been?
I don't need to know.

* * * *

In today's mailbox
alongside ads and bills:
a shrinking spider.

* * * *

Just past the window
hungry turtledoves! Any
word from my master?

* * * *

Last night I couldn't
get to sleep again. My cat
kept watch over me.

* * * *

"I don't love you now."
An indicative sentence.
Simple, like the rest.

* * * *

Rain mixed with snow? Snow
mixed with rain? A rook calmly
hops across the field.

* * * *

A blackbird watches
me severely: what have I
forgotten this time?

* * * *

World in a dewdrop.
In seventeen syllables
Issa's vast haiku.

* * * *

Good morning, sparrow!
Was it you I saw last year
in late December?

Came of It

I stayed silent for many years.
Nothing came of it—

neither good,
nor evil.

FEBRUARY 2005

May 10, 2008

A girl
in a short T-shirt
and the low-riding jeans
that they're still wearing
this season

smiles
shyly for the camera

The stranger
she approached a moment earlier
takes
her picture
in front of the ornate
little doors (art deco?),
opened wide before

a crematory oven
in Mauthausen

Last Night

… als ein Kranich
       –P. C.

Last night I visited your sleep
in a crane's shape.

(You won't remember it when you wake,
you can't remember it—
one always remembers differently from the other,
one always feels it differently.)

Why a crane? I don't know.
But I desired you, though I don't even know
if I was a man.
(Besides you had
your own.)

What did I do? Nothing, only called mutely
in the predawn mist,
behind the seven mountains,
behind the seven forests
that grew then
between you and me,
behind the seven-armed rivers of the fates—

in yours, or mine: I don't

know?

Yes, I Am

For many days now
I've been walking back
through hazy Krakow
but I'm not yet home
from the pink sand
and pink limestone
of my Jerusalem.

I'm still returning
to the Wailing Wall.

I still wander
in the narrow labyrinth
of the Via Dolorosa.

Sometimes
the gap above my head
reveals the moon

still full.

I still wander
in the beginning.

Are you a Jew?
an old Hasidim asks,
probably younger than I am.

Yes, I'm a poet—
I want to say for once

but I just smile
and answer:

Shalom, achi!

Acknowledgments

Poems in this collection have appeared, sometimes in different versions, in the following collections and journals: Ryszard Krynicki, *Citizen R.K. Does Not Live*, ed. Robert A. Davies, John M. Gogol (Mr. Cogito Press, 1985), *Spoiling Cannibals' Fun: Poetry of the Last Two Decades of Communist Rule*, ed. and with translations by Stanisław Barańczak and Clare Cavanagh (Northwestern University Press, 1991), *The Arkansas International, Chicago Review, Common Knowledge, Little Star, The Manhattan Review, Metamorphoses, The New Republic, Ploughshares*, and *Triquarterly*.

This volume has been a long time coming. I was Stanisław Barańczak's graduate research assistant in the early eighties when he first asked me to help him with Ryszard Krynicki's poems. Stanisław and Ania Barańczak gave me a home in Polish poetry, and my debts to Krystyna and Ryszard Krynicki are almost as great. My thanks are also due to Tadeusz Nyczek, who explained various politico-linguistic puns and then checked the English-language results for missed jokes and mistakes, to my new publisher Barbara Epler, and to my longtime editor and friend Drenka Willen. Thanks, finally, to my family, Mike and Martin Lopez.

New Directions Paperbooks—a partial listing

Martín Adán, The Cardboard House
César Aira, Ema, the Captive
  An Episode in the Life of a Landscape Painter
  Ghosts
Will Alexander, The Sri Lankan Loxodrome
Paul Auster, The Red Notebook
Honoré de Balzac, Colonel Chabert
Djuna Barnes, Nightwood
Charles Baudelaire, The Flowers of Evil*
Bei Dao, City Gate, Open Up
Nina Berberova, The Ladies From St. Petersburg
Max Blecher, Adventures in Immediate Irreality
Roberto Bolaño, By Night in Chile
  Distant Star
  Last Evenings on Earth
  Nazi Literature in the Americas
Jorge Luis Borges, Labyrinths
  Professor Borges
  Seven Nights
Coral Bracho, Firefly Under the Tongue*
Kamau Brathwaite, Ancestors
Basil Bunting, Complete Poems
Anne Carson, Antigonick
  Glass, Irony & God
Horacio Castellanos Moya, Senselessness
Louis-Ferdinand Céline
  Death on the Installment Plan
  Journey to the End of the Night
Rafael Chirbes, On the Edge
Inger Christensen, alphabet
Jean Cocteau, The Holy Terrors
Peter Cole, The Invention of Influence
Julio Cortázar, Cronopios & Famas
Albert Cossery, The Colors of Infamy
Robert Creeley, If I Were Writing This
Guy Davenport, 7 Greeks
Osamu Dazai, No Longer Human
H.D., Tribute to Freud
  Trilogy
Helen DeWitt, The Last Samurai
Robert Duncan, Selected Poems
Eça de Queirós, The Maias
William Empson, 7 Types of Ambiguity
Shusaku Endo, Deep River
Jenny Erpenbeck, The End of Days
  Visitation
Lawrence Ferlinghetti
  A Coney Island of the Mind

F. Scott Fitzgerald, The Crack-Up
  On Booze
Forrest Gander, The Trace
Henry Green, Pack My Bag
Allen Grossman, Descartes' Loneliness
John Hawkes, Travesty
Felisberto Hernández, Piano Stories
Hermann Hesse, Siddhartha
Takashi Hiraide, The Guest Cat
Yoel Hoffman, Moods
Susan Howe, My Emily Dickinson
  That This
Bohumil Hrabal, I Served the King of England
Sonallah Ibrahim, That Smell
Christopher Isherwood, The Berlin Stories
Fleur Jaeggy, Sweet Days of Discipline
Alfred Jarry, Ubu Roi
B.S. Johnson, House Mother Normal
James Joyce, Stephen Hero
Franz Kafka, Amerika: The Man Who Disappeared
John Keene, Counternarratives
Laszlo Krasznahorkai, Satantango
  The Melancholy of Resistance
  Seiobo There Below
Eka Kurniawan, Beauty Is a Wound
Rachel Kushner, The Strange Case of Rachel K
Mme. de Lafayette, The Princess of Clèves
Lautréamont, Maldoror
Sylvia Legris, The Hideous Hidden
Denise Levertov, Selected Poems
Li Po, Selected Poems
Clarice Lispector, The Hour of the Star
  Near to the Wild Heart
  The Passion According to G. H.
Federico García Lorca, Selected Poems*
  Three Tragedies
Nathaniel Mackey, Splay Anthem
Stéphane Mallarmé, Selected Poetry and Prose*
Norman Manea, Captives
Javier Marías, Your Face Tomorrow (3 volumes)
Bernadette Mayer, Works & Days
Thomas Merton, New Seeds of Contemplation
  The Way of Chuang Tzu
Henri Michaux, Selected Writings
Dunya Mikhail, The War Works Hard
Henry Miller, The Colossus of Maroussi
  Big Sur & The Oranges of Hieronymus Bosch

Yukio Mishima, Confessions of a Mask
  Death in Midsummer
Eugenio Montale, Selected Poems*
Vladimir Nabokov, Laughter in the Dark
  Nikolai Gogol
  The Real Life of Sebastian Knight
Raduan Nassar, A Cup of Rage
Pablo Neruda, The Captain's Verses*
  Love Poems*
  Residence on Earth*
Charles Olson, Selected Writings
George Oppen, New Collected Poems
Wilfred Owen, Collected Poems
Michael Palmer, The Laughter of the Sphinx
Nicanor Parra, Antipoems*
Boris Pasternak, Safe Conduct
Kenneth Patchen
  Memoirs of a Shy Pornographer
Octavio Paz, Selected Poems
  A Tale of Two Gardens
Victor Pelevin, Omon Ra
Saint-John Perse, Selected Poems
René Philoctete, Massacre River
Ezra Pound, The Cantos
  New Selected Poems and Translations
Raymond Queneau, Exercises in Style
Qian Zhongshu, Fortress Besieged
Raja Rao, Kanthapura
Herbert Read, The Green Child
Kenneth Rexroth, Selected Poems
Keith Ridgway, Hawthorn & Child
Rainer Maria Rilke
  Poems from the Book of Hours
Arthur Rimbaud, Illuminations*
  A Season in Hell and The Drunken Boat*
Guillermo Rosales, The Halfway House
Evelio Rosero, The Armies
Fran Ross, Oreo
Joseph Roth, The Emperor's Tomb
  The Hundred Days
  The Hotel Years
Raymond Roussel, Locus Solus
Ihara Saikaku, The Life of an Amorous Woman
Nathalie Sarraute, Tropisms
Albertine Sarrazin, Astragal
Jean-Paul Sartre, Nausea
  The Wall
Delmore Schwartz
  In Dreams Begin Responsibilities

W. G. Sebald, The Emigrants
  The Rings of Saturn
  Vertigo
Aharon Shabtai, J'accuse
Hasan Shah, The Dancing Girl
C. H. Sisson, Selected Poems
Stevie Smith, Best Poems
Gary Snyder, Turtle Island
Muriel Spark, The Driver's Seat
  The Girls of Slender Means
  Memento Mori
George Steiner, My Unwritten Books
Antonio Tabucchi, Indian Nocturne
  Pereira Maintains
Junichiro Tanizaki, A Cat, a Man & Two Women
Yoko Tawada, Memoirs of a Polar Bear
Dylan Thomas, A Child's Christmas in Wales
  Collected Poems
  Under Milk Wood
Uwe Timm, The Invention of Curried Sausage
Charles Tomlinson, Selected Poems
Tomas Tranströmer
  The Great Enigma: New Collected Poems
Leonid Tsypkin, Summer in Baden-Baden
Tu Fu, Selected Poems
Frederic Tuten, The Adventures of Mao
Regina Ullmann, The Country Road
Jane Unrue, Love Hotel
Paul Valéry, Selected Writings
Enrique Vila-Matas, Bartleby & Co.
  Vampire in Love
Elio Vittorini, Conversations in Sicily
Rosmarie Waldrop, Gap Gardening
Robert Walser, The Assistant
  Microscripts
  The Tanners
Wang An-Shih, The Late Poems
Eliot Weinberger, The Ghosts of Birds
Nathanael West, The Day of the Locust
  Miss Lonelyhearts
Tennessee Williams, Cat on a Hot Tin Roof
  The Glass Menagerie
  A Streetcar Named Desire
William Carlos Williams, In the American Grain
  Selected Poems
  Spring and All
Mushtaq Ahmed Yousufi, Mirages of the Mind
Louis Zukofsky, "A"
  Anew

*BILINGUAL EDITION

For a complete listing, request a free catalog from New Directions, 80 8th Avenue, New York, NY 10011
or visit us online at ndbooks.com